Glimpses of Eternity

Glimpses of Eternity

☙

ALESSIO PERRY

RESOURCE *Publications* · Eugene, Oregon

GLIMPSES OF ETERNITY

Resource Publications
An Imprint of Wipf and Stock Publishers
199 W. 8th Ave., Suite 3
Eugene, OR 97401

www.wipfandstock.com

PAPERBACK ISBN: 979-8-3852-6709-5
HARDCOVER ISBN: 979-8-3852-6710-1
EBOOK ISBN: 979-8-3852-6711-8

To all believers

Contents

Contents

Preface

GLIMPSES OF ETERNITY HAS been a long time in the making. I composed the first poem—*Cosmopolitan*—ten years ago. I was then about to undertake a journey which would have led me to discover unforeseen shores; it is along this path of life, at different stages and at different times, that all these poems, like beads on a string, have come to see the light.

This small collection aims to remind us of something we too often tend to forget in our 'busy', modern lives: that it's in simple things and small details that the Divine dwells. Everything is simply just a reflection of that Inner Source which underpins everything and everyone. Hence why all these poems are littered with symbols: from nature to feelings, from ancient myths to mundane objects such as a lamppost or a passport, I have been catching glimpses of the Source along the way in the most disparate things. After all, everything can be a source for meditation and contemplation. But not everything may be as simple as it seems at first glimpse: likewise, some verses can hold more than one meaning. Punctuation is key; and capitalised words too encapsulate deeper meanings.

A great source of inspiration for *Glimpses of Eternity* has been the Italian poet Giuseppe Ungaretti (1888–1970). A soldier fighting in the Alpine trenches during the First World War, Ungaretti wrote brief, highly symbolic rhymes on every scrap of paper he could lay his hands on. This lack of space helped Ungaretti to condense his message in very few, powerful sentences; so much so that one of his most famous poems is only four words long! Sometime you can say much with very little; this is probably one of Unga-retti's most enduring legacies.

Another influence on this collection has been the poetry of Giovanni Pascoli (1855–1912), especially his early collection *Myricae*—both for its focus on 'humble' topics and the natural world, and for the brevity of its compositions (a revolution for Italian literature at the time).

I want to reserve a separate mention for the so-called "Japa-nese waka-style" poems. This poetic style first originated in China, and was later adopted in Japan during the Heian period (ca. 794–1185). Each composition consists of five lines for a total of 31 syllables, in a 5–7–5–7–7 pattern. Due to their very short na-ture, such poems are ideal to depict specific, symbolically charged scenes . In doing so, I have followed in the steps of those monks who, among many others, also adopted this particular style as it was ideal to express *yugen*—that is, "mystery and depth". In my case, Nature is the protagonist and the starting point for a deeper journey of introspection and meditation on topics such as the di-vine, life, and death.

All these poems are meant to be read aloud; each of them has a different cadence to it, which also reflects their inner nature. Hence poems like *The Scotsman* sound more vibrant, whereas *Grave* and *Grain of dust* conjure up a more reflective, dream-like mood.

I hope that this humble collection may be a source of enjoy-ment and contemplation and that may give you inspiration to catch your own 'glimpses of Eternity'.

Cosmopolitan

I am a traveller.
My path is Life.
My luggage is my experiences.
My jewels, my friends.
My home is Earth, Sky is my roof.
My destination: Infinity.

Enlightenment

That secret Sun
you carry within
warms you up
with divine Love.

Like a candid lotus
from mud sprung up,
your soul to Heaven
through a mindful life.

You reap what you sow

You reap what you sow:
it's a natural law.
Fair, equal, and just;
sometime all this
makes people aghast.

But you have nothing
to be surprised of;
it's a natural law,
the product of that
Eternal Love.

Don't ask for forgiveness
where there hasn't been any.
Don't look for understanding
when there has been none.

It's a wheel that spins,
and turns, and runs;
it's a natural law,
to reap what you sow.

Wish

Deep within
the still centre
of my being,
may I find
Peace.

Silently within
the calmness
of the grove,
may I share
Peace.

Gently within
the greater circle
of humankind,
may I radiate
Peace.

Life

I am a rose.
I open up,
my dewy, feeble
petals kissed by
the morning Sun.

I leave my roots,
a strong wind
carries me upwards.
It's a storm.

Tossed here and there,
I float up and down,
aimless. I feel lost,
I do not know the Way.
Black clouds frighten me.

But then colors start to
speckle the dark slate;
what could this mean?
"It's the Rainbow you see."

The rain depletes,
the winds calm down;
and I, sleeping deep,
pass under the shiny gown.

A veil lifts up:
it's sky blue there.
The breeze, now gentle,
pushes me with care.

Here I am today,
a safe shore reached;
tomorrow, who knows,
nor I care one bit.

One day I will wilt,
of that only I am sure;
for now I live on,
every day a new dawn.

Navigating

I am a sailor
in the midst of
this sea of Life.
The route
at the moment
is untracked.
I do not know
what awaits me,
nor have I a map.
My steps, unknown;
only Faith have I got.
Faith in knowing
that whatever
needs to happen
will happen, as it
has happened thus far.
Hence worry not:
just sail with the flow.

Liberation

Fly, fly high
small, big Heart;
the Sky embraces
your splendor.

Bright pathways
in front of you
at once disappear,
by emptiness filled.

But the Way
is not lost;
forever it shines
within yourself.

Pensive as I was

Pensive as I was
in the depths of the night,
little did I realize
you were coming forthright.
"Look, the Sun rises!"
"How's that possible?,"
I cried. "Don't you see we are
in the midst of the night?"

"But Light is here
for you to see,
even when you think
you cannot see it.
Look for it.
Feel it.
Embrace it.
Shine."

Breeze

The sound of the waves
gently rustling in my ears
takes me away
to times gone by.

The warm southern breeze
caressing my hair
takes me away
to places long lost.

The creamy full globe
adorning the heavens
takes me to deserts
far, far away.

Sitting on the beach,
a tear on my cheek
reminds me of how
truly old I am.

Rumbling, crumbling wave

Rumbling, crumbling wave,
dash against
these rocky knaves.

Hit, splash and crash;
a perlaceous foam
sparks up in the sky.

Retreat, but it's not
the end; always forward,
again, and again.

Peaceful Being

Gazing out of my window,
birds chirping in the woods;
rain drizzling down finely,
dawn pinking up my room.

Sipping cloud-mist tea,
the dewy peonies glitter;
like pearls in an ocean green,
I lose myself within it.

Under the olive tree

Under the olive tree
cross-legged I sat,
back leant on the trunk,
gaze up to the Sun.

A gentle breeze rustled
through the leaves, giving
them shapes which
made my heart ache.

A mighty eagle perched
on the shoulders of
a golden-cupped ephebe;

how much I wish I could
serve the immortals on
their ethereal thrones!

Another day

Someone jogging,
music playing.
Crows scavenging,
foes at bay.

War rages around me;
within me is stillness.

I am shut in my world,
retired from events;
life goes on unscathed,
philosophy is my bread.

Grave

I would pay loftly
to be buried softly
whilst sipping tea smoothly
surrounded by fellows who,
with their poems, rend me jolly;
with parchment in hand,
I'd be buried gladly
even under Italic sand.

Grain of dust

I am a grain of dust
lightly speckled with lust
in a dream which must
come to an end someday;

if there ever were a way
to keep all this going
perhaps I would be trying,
though then I'd miss Myself.

Halved

(dedicated to my beloved)

In the morning,
no smell of your coffee
in the kitchen.

No watching TV
together on the sofa
at night.

The pillow, the house, my world,
All so empty,
All so forlorn.

Yearning every moment
to be complete
again.

The cosmopolitan's enemy

Red, black, green or blue;
it doesn't really matter the hue.
Its aim is always the same:
to make the lot of us half lame.

Wherefore I cannot espouse that;
as the world is my home,
every culture like my own,
a passport is not part of my pack.

The Scotsman

Hailing down from the glen
swirling tartan, fair mystique,
firmly advancing with proud physique
here now comes my Scotsman.

How enthralled now I feel
as he draws near and near;
his longing eyes, of a faint green hue
make me burn like anew.

Hugging him, his lips on mine,
a thousand stars around me shine;
but as he leaves, bidding goodbye,
there's not much else for me but cry.

Hope

Scented candlelight
in purple twilight.

Smoky clouds
dancing on earth.

Here I wonder
what I deserve;

may it be
one day all
Clear.

A late summer evening

Incipient dusk.
A solitary lamppost
amidst church and graves.

Silence fills the air;
surrounded by leafy sentinels,
here I find my peace.

On Odin's wings

The ravens of wisdom
spin through the Earth,
carrying fair news
back to their berth.

The Allfather oversees
every deed on land and sea;
over Freja's blossoms, over Njord's fields,
the Allfather's ravens gather much yield.

From ice-frozen mountains
down green, shady glens;
along coasts, in fountains,
in all the Allfather blends.

Oh mead of poetry, most blessed of drinks!
May you and the Allfather keep me away from the brink.
For there's only three things that I can wish for:
Odin's love, and wisdom, and ever-truthful lore.

Eternal Spring

(Japanese 'waka' style)

Dewy, golden cups
Zesty fragrance ascending
An emerald sea

Without any horizon
An infinity within

Paradise

(Japanese 'waka' style)

White-rosy petals
Ripe golden globes, hanging low
On a verdant sea

A sense of tranquillity;
Frisk breeze, carrying inner peace

On the Irish Sea

(Japanese 'waka' style)

Billowing mist veil;
Gliding on the azure slate
with mystic silence.

Visions on the horizon,
ploughing the veil through and through.

Release

(Japanese 'waka' style)

In eerie silence
Sudden flash in the grey vault
Booming and cracking

A water wall tumbling down; peace
shattered, energy released.

Isarfjördur

(Japanese 'waka' style)

An enchanted world,
home to trolls, fairies and gods
under mist-capped giants;

their mossy coats, drizzle-soaked,
wrapping up their hearts of stone.

Sound of Mull

(Japanese 'waka' style)

Hail, the purple hills!
Pine trees clutching on gentle slopes
beside ruined castles.

Heather vibrating with life,
water still like death in graves.

Lake Myvatn

(Japanese 'waka' style)

In glacial waters
a solitary pillar
propping up the sky;

sparrows hunting in the clouds,
breathing in gnarly wild thyme.

Crisp Autumn night

Crisp Autumn night,
filled with delights,
your shiny stars glitter
like diamonds on velvet.

Crisp Autumn night,
so quiet, and yet so bright,
your breeze among the leaves
carries whispers from the Gods.

Crisp Autumn night,
that sees me here to write,
I thank Heaven for thee,
for bringing much Clarity.

30

Veiled moonlight,
mist floating;
wand'ring crows,
pines singing.

Tasting Scotch
in candlelight,
people fretting
I'm alone.

Fools.
It's just another round
'round the Sun;
how can I possible be
doomed?

All is right
here with me.

Out in the woods

At the fringe of society,
out in the woods,
I live at the edge
among trees and roods.

Being out of the schemes,
I am shunned, cast away;
it's for what I don't say,
don't do, but mean.

And yet joy fills me
from the lofty peaks of mind
down to my core's inner caves.
And so I say this to thee:

Take heed of such lore;
and you'll reach a different shore.

Lounge view

(Japanese 'waka' style)

A human river,
arising and descending
on titanic birds.

Many places on the screen,
only one Destination.

www.ingramcontent.com/pod-product-compliance
Lightning Source LLC
Chambersburg PA
CBHW060634030426
42337CB00018B/3351